Why? Are We Crumbling From Within?

J. Gordon Monson and Jim Monson

Published by J. Gordon Monson, 2021.

I0426871

DEDICATION

I dedicate this writing, as well as, give thanks and honor to all those brave men and women, both past and present, in our Mighty Arm Forces, as well as, in those
People in Blue who have served in the past, and are now serving to keep us all safe from all domestic and foreign invasions, threats, and illegal trespasses.

TABLE OF CONTENT

Forewords:

This foreword is a important reminder to all who read and ponder it. It is our Nation's moto. It can still be found on every coin and paper currency produced by the U. S. Treasury. It's same money we all carry with us whenever we go about our activities every day: That moto is:

IN GOD WE TRUST.

Testimonials:

The last instruction, or commandment that the Lord Jesus Christ gave to His Disciples, as well as, to all of us:

And Jesus came and spoke to them, saying, "All authority has been given to Me in heaven and on the earth. Go therefore and make disciples of all nations, baptizing them in the name of the Father and the Son and of the Holy Spirit. Teaching them to observe all things that I have commanded you; and lo, I am with you always, even to the end of the age," Amen

Matthew 28:18 – 20 NKJV

This is a promise and message directly from The Word of God of all of His creation, to us all:

"For God so loved the world that He gave His only begotten Son, that whoever believes in Him should not perish but have everlasting life. For God did not send His Son into the world to condemn the world, but that the world through Him might be saved."

John 3:16 – 17 NKJV

Prologue

To our Nation's Elected Leadership:

I'm starting this off with my personal complaints. My hope is that many of our fellow citizens read and agree, and that you in elected leadership will read this first part, and then agree with me as well. Then I hope you will continue to read my final summation in the last few pages of this writing.

I believe we all should be willing to be outspoken and to make certain recommendations to each of you for changes that will first show all those who are in leadership of our still great country that we mean business about our concerns. The following is a list of my complaints: I'm tired of all the unnecessary spending; of our government mandates in every area of our lives; of their proposal to change our energy sources; for this proposed, far-reaching, expensive, green new deal; for the one group rule in some states, and now in our federal government with no safe guards to stop extreme agenda changes and rulings; for the long standing threat to the most innocent lives; for the growing losses in our freedoms of worship, some call it a war against Christianity; for taxation without regard for where the money is spent; for a threat to our first and second amendment rights, as well as, a disregard by some of you for all the other amendments; for the far reaching lack of concern for the huge National debt; for the blatant disregard for our election integrity, and for so very much more.

One Citizen's Observances

I wrote this after witnessing from a distance the events that took place a few days before, and then for many days after our general elections on November 3rd, 2020. We saw too many of our 50 states do very last minute changes to their own election policies. Some of these changes were made by their state's governors or by their own attorney generals. Other states made changes done through the court system. However, none of these election policy changes were done by the individual state's elected congress, the governing authority in this matter as is required in the U. S. Constitution. According to the U. S. Constitution each state can change their own state's election policies only by the authorization given to the full elected congress of their individual state.

Further, the Tenth Amendment gives each state further protection from actions taken by the Federal Government. This information is shown below:

The Tenth Amendment to the U. S. Constitution reads: Each state retains its sovereignty, freedom and independence, and every power, jurisdiction and right, which is not by this Confederation expressly delegated to the United States, in congress assembled.

Judicial interpretation:

The Tenth Amendment, which makes explicit the idea that the federal government is limited to only the powers granted in the

Constitution, has been declared to be a truism[1]by the Supreme Court. In *United States v. Sprague*[2](1931) the Supreme Court[3]asserted that the amendment "added nothing to the [Constitution] as originally ratified"

State's Authority

This interpretation of the Tenth Amendment tells us that the states have granted authority, and have given it to the Federal Government with limitations of consent. Should the Federal Government overstep this authority given to it by the states corporately, or even individually, the states have sovereignty to overrule any passage that the Federal Government might take. There are steps to overrule the Federal Government now taking place today. To date this year, as of this writing, two states have approved the reversal the U. S. Supreme Court ruling made in 1973, Roe VS Wade. This reversal is to be only within their state's own geographic boundaries. These two states have overturned the highly controversial ruling regarding abortion, disallowing such actions of abortion within their own state boundaries.

There are also many other areas passed either by an act of the U. S. Congress or by executive order by the current President, where individual states in their own sovereignty given them under this Ten Amendment can and could choose to reverse any federal laws or executive orders imposed upon their state's own people. These same protections given can include the individual state's rights regarding any actions by the federal government that a state, or states feel oversteps the federal government's authority. The states can stand on the Tenth Amendment to overrule federal abuses within the borders of their own state. If the Federal Government fails in their duties to protect the citizens of their individual state from both foreign and domestic invasions, each state, the property owners, and also the local county has the right to place barriers, fencing or walls to ensure the safety of their own citizens from these type of intrusion, threats and trespass from anyone or anything that violates their right of privacy, safety and losses. Beyond that these same people, the county within the state, and/or the individual state should then have the right to invoice the Federal Government for all costs realized by the person, county and state for installing barriers, fencing, or even walls correcting the failure of the protection required by the Federal Government to ensure the safety of their own U. S. citizens.

Also this Tenth Amendment to the U. S. Constitution should give each state protection from rules passed by the Federal Government regarding the state's right to educate their own students. Each state should be able, under the guidance of this amendment, to put in place whatever school systems they choose, called freedom of school choice, without losing any of the funding that comes directly from the U. S. Department of Education. These school choices should include Charter schools, Christian schools, and/or Religious schools, as long as they teach the basic curriculum of reading, writing and arithmetic, without denying them the right to Biblical teaching, and/or including sport programs, musical and drama programs.

First Summary

So, to summarize, this tenth Amendment is yet another protection provided, which also includes the First and Second Amendments, along with every other vital protection put in place by the brilliance of our Nation's Founding Fathers that ensure our people within each state have immunity from any possible tyrannical actions taken by our Federal Government. Actions which will or can deprive our freedoms, censorship of free speech, or violate any other precious freedoms given to each U. S. citizen under the guidelines and protections assured us in our U. S. Constitution and U. S. Bill of Rights.

If we all agree that the U.S. Constitution and our U. S. Bill of rights are our Nation's final authority, then we must conclude that this is the rule of law in which we must base all necessary judgements and actions. We should also conclude that any other method of changing the election policy(ies) done by any other method, or any other body was done in error, and then the error must be dealt with appropriate corrective actions by that separate individual state's elected congressional body.

Since each separate State in our Nation is sovereign and independent from other states and from the Federal Government in accordance with the U. S. Constitution, and all the Amendments, only each separate State's elected Congressional body, as a whole, has the authority to make changes to their own State's election policies, as well as, to their State's school programs, and any other matter which can adversely affect their citizens. These cannot be changed without the concurrence of each State's whole elected Congressional body. Realizing this fact, it can limit the actions taken by the Federal Government, which can be a very good thing to put some needed checks and necessary safeguards on what is passed by the U. S. Congress and U.S. Senate.

Effects of Partisan News Reporting

Where were most of the news people when downtown Portland, Oregon was nearly destroyed from what most of the news reporting agencies stated to be mostly peaceful demonstrations? These ongoing riotous, destructive activities lasted for over one hundred straight nights without a pause. One unnamed news reporting agency had their reporter standing in camera view of a store building ablaze with fire, and in his verbal report he said, "These are mostly peaceful protests." When the camera turned in another direction the video showed two male rioter dressed in dark clothing using bats or clubs to break two other storefront windows, and other men in dark attire were running from another store carrying merchandise. These were obviously not items they had purchased from that store as they could be seen running out through a shattered glass door, and because of all the wanton destruction going on around them at that same moment.

Today a big part of downtown Portland, Oregon is still showing signs of the mass destruction that took place. There are building after building with boarded up window openings and graffiti. Many of these stores are now out of business. The owners were either forced to close down, or they were forced to move on to what might be a safer location. Yet, we still hear reports of the nighttime rioters still doing their destruction in their city. But the rioters have moved on to other parts in their city where they still can do their evil deeds. Where there is still windows to break and merchandise to loot. The massive destruction has given the whole once beautiful Rose City a dirty mangled face and black eyes through most of downtown.

At last count there have been close to three hundred occasions for riotous, destructive activities in the dark of night taking place in several of our American cities. Of that count almost one third of them are done in Portland, Oregon.

But, our question still goes unanswered, "Where are all the Main Stream Media reporting agencies? Why are they not going out to at least to report on human interest stories regarding the adverse effects on people who have had their livelihood taken from them with such needless, senseless activities, and the huge costs of economic losses? One has to question if this is another intentional 'sin of omissions' on the part of these news reporting agencies? Doesn't it matter that these terrible violent, destructive activities are even more important to all their viewing audience than who is getting their vaccinations, or what some well-known sport figure or entertainer has to say about any given subject, or even what the governor of some state across the country thinks is the best way to fight the ongoing, challenging pandemic in his state?

I dare not weigh in on the partisan politics areas of news reporting, only to say that it is far too one sided. The facts are that most of their reporting has been swayed for too many of the viewing public who believe these reported stories. Too many of these stories are worded in such a way to benefit one group over the other groups by upwards of 70 to 80%. And, when any of their reports are proven to be incorrect, then where are their retractions? They are simply not to be found. The viewers in our great country deserve fair, accurate and unbiased reporting, and without omission of any whole or parts of critical news worthy stories.

Questions

1. What are some of the things you personally are afraid of?
2. Why are there so many slanted news reports that gives only what they want you to know, often omitting some or all of the truth, or often ignoring some important stories or events because they don't fit within their narratives?
3. Why is there such a Fear for the loss of freedom of speech, and for selective censorship of certain individuals by news and by big tech groups?
4. Why is our current Government leadership doing some outlandish scary activities that often either circumvent the U. S. Constitution or disregard some of our privacy standards?
5. Why do some of our elected leadership take advantage of the double standards, and why are these condoned, or ignored by many

MSM? (Main Stream media)

1. Why are there some deceptive practices done by some leaders to mandate some selective, business shut downs, which have proven to be mostly worthless?

I encourage you to add your own list of some of the things you are afraid of, and then make them known to all those who have authority to make corrections?

List of Can Do's

My various subjects found below contain what we individuals can and should do to make the Nation's leadership know about our concerns.

The following several paragraphs are messages to our Nation's elected leadership on both sides of the isle, as well as, to any concerned citizens of our great country.

This writing is after the 2020 general election. The count shows that the republicans won most of the elections around the country, with one of the few exceptions being the presidential race. The presidential incumbent was ahead when I went to bed close to midnight on the 3rd of November. However, early the next morning the news reports showed that somehow the challenger had made some substantial gains in the middle of the night, and was then leading in all the eight swing states. The history tells us a republican incumbent had never lost a race while carrying both the Florida, Ohio, and Iowa races, and then that morning the incumbent was still yet leading out of over 2,700 counties nationwide the by a margin of upwards of 70 percent of them. In the down races the republicans gain almost one and one half dozen seats in the House of Representatives, while the Democrats stayed about even with the GOP in the Senate races, with two Georgia races going into a runoff set for

January 5th, 2021. In that runoff the Democrats eventually took both of these seats in the Senate leaving the balance of power even, but with the new vice president to be the tie breaker.

Defying all the odds and ratios in the general election when all the votes were counted in the presidential election the Democrat challenger won in all eight of the swing states either by some middle of the night miracle, or by some very questionable actions happening in the wee hours of the night or early on the morning of November 4th, 2020.

I have my own opinion on what happened in the general election, in the presidential race, however, I have not personally seen any of the evidence that many claim exists in those swing states, except for the suspicious video in the count from Atlanta Georgia area showing some activity after most of the crew had left for the night. I'll leave all that happened for the professionals to investigate. One thing is certain, many on both sides feel that something was very wrong in several of the swing states, and that something unjust happened during the election in middle of the night, or very early the next morning.

My next question is should we have gone forward with installing new leadership with so many of these highly suspicious questions still unanswered, or even at least investigated by a neutral body. If I were either of the candidates in the presidential race, or any other race with so many questions, I would want to know that I won or lost the race fair and square. That would be my challenge to each of the interested parties, and I encourage you all to get the answers to insure we are doing the fair and sure justice to all the questionable clouds hanging over this last election process, and with these gone unanswered with a complete investigation.

Division by Conflict and Accusations

The next subject is the serious division, conflict, accusations of wrong doing, and downright hatred directed at our sitting President of these (supposedly) United States of America during the last four years. I'm puzzled and shocked by some of the actions of some of your members in both the House and Senate, and by what a number of you have been doing and saying. It appears some of you were deliberately attempting to undermine everything that our last president and his administration were trying to accomplish, whether good or bad, during these last four years. If they had been going in the wrong directions, and if his administration was doing things that were bad for our people, then I could understand why you might be in disagreement with them. But, the degree of opposition, the combativeness, and the name calling towards him and his administration have been both unjust, uncalled for, lacking statesmanship, as well as, without precedent. These actions by some of you have been so extreme that they have been foundational in the reasons our Nation's people are modeling the same division displayed by your actions. These examples you all set, along with those outside of government who have an agenda and are willing to fund anti-American activities, are another reason why we have such great amounts of division within our Nation.

To get answers for any doubts about what 'We The People' see is that This President and his administration have done in the last four years, please read the following list. They have accomplished some amazing things for us even though they have had an uphill battle in every move they have made. The gains are hard to dispute. They start with the best economy we have seen in decades, with the lowest unemployment numbers; the most people working in the African American, the Latino, women in the work force, and young under thirties groups. The record high stock market gains; the tax revenues which were up; along with the confidence of the people for most all of the last four years. The gains in Middle-East with four countries signing peace agreements with Israel. Plus the promise that more would sign, if given more time. The fact that we are not at war, nor have started any other wars during this four year time period are just some of the gains we made during the last four years.

Then our last President took on the Southern border crisis. It remains unsettled, however, we have made vast improvements with the hundreds of miles of wall making our country more safe and secure. The President also had worked with Mexico leadership to have them co-operate in keeping most of the people from coming across our southern border to harm us, or take away so many of our jobs, as well as, to bring in various diseases.

Why would so many of you fight against him, and against what is right with all the success that has been accomplished at our southern border, as well as, other areas that are getting better? Is it only because you didn't like the man who was in the oval office at the time?

Then there are the improvements in balancing tariffs in trade with several countries, and again, the hopeful promise of more progress given with still more countries given more time. Our last administration had also been talking trade with China, the biggest elephant in the world, who has for many years taken advantage of us both imbalances in trade tariffs, and also with them stealing our tech. There were ongoing plans for much more progress in all these trade areas if given more time. It was believed that they would have made great gains even with China.

The next subject is the improvement in care of our returning, wounded, military veterans. Care has vastly improved for these warriors by the last administration during the last four years. They opened the option for vets to go to any medical care facility, if they can't gain timely help from the veteran's administration, or if the distance to travel is too far from their homes for them to receive timely medical care.

Then, prior to the pandemic hitting our country and all around the world, our unemployment numbers, the number of people in the work force, was the best it has been for several decades. Also, the past four years they were successful in removing several federal mandated regulations that effected most businesses from being efficient in their operation. These changes had helped make doing business less burdensome and more profitable. It had helped both employers and employees, making life in general easier for all of us Americans.

The above are just a short list of the many improvements we've realized under President Trump's watch. Like it or not, Mr. Trump was your president for the last four years, and he was also mine. His obvious motivation was to do what is right in most all areas that are most important to 'We The People.'

I'm asking for yours and your peers resolve to be supportive, standing shoulder to shoulder, with each administration in their efforts to concentrate on all the various remaining problems we face. We ask that you do all that you can to benefit the people in our great country. I also ask that you solve any and all existing problems long before you bring in any new, untested, costly programs that will further encumber us with higher taxes, and which may or may not benefit all of our people. Next we ask that you all do all that is within your power to put aside all the hurtful partisan bickering; to help bring some sense to what the world sees you doing, in place of the confusing, disruptive, divisive actions we all see going on within the halls of government now.

Some in this administration, as well as, some past administrations have stepped over the line with actions that are considered unethical, unconstitutional, or even illegal. Most were much more compromising than the accusations by some of you alleged against President Trump and his administration. We wonder why so many of you, and even some of the news agencies still are unwilling to accept the proven results of the long, expensive investigation into what was called the Russian Probe, a Conversation by the President with someone in Russia, that has been proven to be totally without problems?

Later only to find out that someone other than Mr. Trump, or any in his administration, were involved in the plot to make him look guilty of something. In other words, this other party was apparently attempting to frame both him and members of his administration back then.

The next question is why do we govern to reward the bad apples, but levy surcharges the good ones? Why should anyone think it is good to reward those who are doing something bad or harmful, or reward someone who expects payment, rewards and support for doing nothing?

We should all want our government to protect us from both foreign and domestic threats. That should be the highest responsibility of our government, yet we see several American cities making moves to partially or fully defund their own police departments. One has to question why we would remove those who have pledged to serve and protect our citizens. If the problem is one or two bad apples among the police force, why not simply remove the bad, and then keep and treasure all the good. Please don't take away funding for our much needed police forces in every city in this country, and please keep all forces and protections in place to protect all of us from the threats that come in unlawfully across our borders every day!

Next we see so many of our cities have become sanctuary cities for those individuals who stole across our Nation's boarders, and who are here without official authorization. We are then offering these same people with benefits that may not even be available to our own citizens.

One has to question why this is happening.

Schools are Changing

The next subject is our schools of higher learning. These have changed over the recent years. They used to be places which encouraged new and innovative ideas, and places where students were allowed to have freedom to think on their own, to expand their knowledge in all areas, and then to prepare each of those college graduates for their own careers out in the workplace. Most of these places of higher learning were founded as institutions of faith. So many were started as Christian based schools, however, today many have moved away from those roots. Their theme seems to have changed towards a different plan. Some of our schools remain open to free thinking, but others are now places of indoctrination, where the theme is to teach the student body to hate our country and hate our longstanding principals of capitalism. Even to hate all the success this method of openness has proven to be for hundreds of years. These decades of past successes have made our country a central for being able and willing to come alongside of those less fortunate than us. To be generous with our resources, not just domestically, but all around the world. We see this shift from the training of our student body in many of these schools. The graduates of the past came out of college with motivations of working hard, where they wanted to become a part of an affluent citizenship. But now too many of our present grads come out not knowing what our country stands for. They are being taught in many of our colleges and universities a different doctrine than in past generations.

That old saying still stands, "If you tell someone a lie often enough, both the speaker and the hearer come to believe it as truth." The result of this method of teaching is giving too many of our students a warped view of our society. It's likely why we find that much of the recent riotous activities in many of our larger cities around the country are done by students from our colleges and universities, who have come alongside, or even leading some other radical minded groups. And, it is suspected that these destructive activities are being funded by some wealthy individuals who have an agenda that includes anti-American values. These movements are totally self-defeating. They go against everything that made our Nation great, and a place where people from other countries wanted to come here to make their home. These demonstrations of riotous activities are also so very costly to our cities, as well as, so disruptive to so many good citizens of our great Nation.

The next subject is our current welfare programs in every state. This is the biggest giveaway program we have. We reward our young unmarried by coming alongside them when they produce a child outside of wedlock, and when they and their families fail to support them. Our government has taken it upon itself to support these individuals for years. It is just one more tax payer funded project that should never been approved all those years ago. We often provide for the unwed mom, or mom and dad, for years before they come off this program. This support should have been by the couple who produced the child, the families, or even churches coming alongside them with short term help, and not we tax payers.

The Giveaway Policies

The next subject is our country's foreign aid program. We've sent hundreds of billions of our tax dollars over the years to so many countries. Why? Are we trying to buy their friendship? Do we ever ask them to pay us back? Maybe even ask them to pay it back with interest?

It's one thing to help a neighbor in need, but quite another thing to continue to give out money year after year to the same recipients with no other logical purpose. This sounds foolish, and is senseless for so many reasons. This is our tax payer moneys, our money, being use for all this spending. Wouldn't it be prudent for all of us to find a way to spend it more wisely? Helping others when they are in need is called benevolence. But, sometimes, when the beneficiary shows no sign of helping themselves, it too becomes like our welfare program. Someone in authority in our leadership needs to step up to do an evaluation to determine who will qualify for our help, and who will not. Our aid should be based upon a temporary assistance policy, and not a permanent handout with no planned end.

The pandemic subject was mentioned earlier, but only briefly. Because of the serious and long term affects it is having on all of us. It's a subject that needs to be addressed in a major, thoughtful discussion. We can speculate all the day long on why the world is suffering with this plague. We don't know if China accidently released it on the rest of the world, or if it was an act of retaliation for the pressures we were putting on them as trading partners. I have my opinion on this, but I don't have facts to back up any speculative theory, so I choose to keep my opinion silent on this. Our country has gone to some great extremes in our efforts to control the spread of this virus, as have most of the countries around the world. Some of these efforts seemed necessary at the time, however, the things that have not worked should be stopped immediately. The social distancing, along with many working from home has helped. Also handwashing and surface disinfecting of all counters and every other surface have been a great benefit. But, shutting down our country for weeks at a time has created more, and bigger problems than they have solved. That, along with the daily panic our news media has promoted has created a loss of public trust in both the media and the experts who are making decisions to try to combat the virus. Also, there are some suspicions about the accuracy of the actual count of the number of deaths directly from this disease. Some believe many victims may have been purposely misreported as covid-19 patients in an effort to make this look worse than it really is. There may be some valid reasons for the medical people and the authorities to do this. I have no proof that this is actually happening, so I choose to not give an opinion.

Then further, there are some states making decisions which defy any sense of reason and logic. Shutting down so many of our businesses, most of them small family run operations, along with closing down so many sporting and other events has added to the total losses, and placed a huge economic strain on our entire country. It may be one that will take years to recover from. Some businesses may never be able to reopen again.

Any deaths, for whatever reason, are unfortunate and devastating to the families, and they deserve our most sincere, heartfelt sympathy.

Next, there are the questions about which businesses are deemed essential and who are non-essential. These decisions made by our governing authorities have so many grey areas. If you were to ask any business owners, or their employees, you would get a definite answer on whose business can be considered essential. Their answer might vary greatly from the people in authority who make these decisions. These shutdowns have had many other adverse side effects. These are so many that naming them all would be impossible in this writing. One certain effect worth mentioning, beyond the economic, is mental health of people. Some people are experiencing depression, suicidal conditions effected by the loss of work and income, and even from a lack of social contact with others.

Then we look at some states and even some countries around the world that choose not to shut down. You will find that their end results are not any different from all the others who decided to shut down for weeks at a time. So, you make the call. Are we doing right by our neighbors, by our citizens, and by our Nation? Can we just work together to make things happen in such a way that no one gets left out? Can we just put our people back to work, as well as, get our kids back to school? And then, we should find that we don't need or expect our government to bail us all out of every situation that comes along? Our history reveals that they don't do this very well. We should never expect them to cover all of our basic needs, because they have neither funding nor ability to do that.

My hope is that all you government leaders at every level see the benefit of working together as committed Statesmen and Stateswomen for the benefit of all the fine people you took that oath to represent and to serve. Also, I hope you will continue reading my Summary and final summary for some ideas to make things work to the benefit of all of our people.

Part 1: Brief History of our Origin

The history lesson and summary below is for all to read. It may have some subjects that are repetitious from above, but each bears repeating to emphasize the most important points.

From 1775 to 1783 our Nation fought against the control and dominance of the British Empire. The people who had relocated here felt they were being very poorly represented. They called it "Taxation without representation." Hence, the famous historical Tea Party event in 1773 when some citizens threw the bags of imported tea, shipped here most likely from England into the Boston Harbor. These people had come over to this new land originally because of the government authority had mandated how they were to practice their religion. Those who came over by ship to this new land wanted the freedom to worship their God however they choose. They also wanted freedom to establish a new Nation without the controls forced upon them from overseas, and one additional reason was high taxation required from Great Brittan.

These brave pioneers established the original thirteen separate colonies which were later changed to states. As they grew, they added more states, usually one at a time. Our latest count is fifty states, including Hawaii and Alaska. We have also added some territories to the list. These include American Samoa, Guam, Northern Mariana Islands, Puerto Rico, and Virgin Islands. And, in recent years we have even entertained the possibility of splitting some of our existing U. S. states in half or in thirds. This has not happened, but many citizens from both Northern California and Southern Oregon have talked about doing this to their states. They have even named the new possible state as the State of Jefferson. These citizens oppose some of the many recent state government regulations imposed on them, along with their objections of how their states spend their tax dollars. These differences are mostly between liberal and conservative thinking people with so many issues and differing agendas.

So you see, by reading the last part of the last paragraph, not much has changed in the time since our Nation was founded. Men have not always agreed on issues both back then and present day.

Solomon, the writer of at least three books in the Bible, was believed to be the wisest mortal man to ever live. He wrote so many of the Proverbs, along with the book of Ecclesiastes and The Song of Solomon. One verse he wrote comes to mind, "There is nothing new under the sun." So, we find that men's differences go back far beyond the two hundred plus years our Nation has existed. There is yet another writing in the book of Matthew in the Bible that is pertinent to our present-day. These are Jesus own words, "Every kingdom divided against itself is brought to desolation, and every city or house divided against itself will not stand." Is that where our (country) (our Nation) is heading today?

Please tell me what you think.

Part 2: History

There were 56 signers of the U.S. Constitution and The Bill of Rights. These were mostly men of faith. Some were pastors and others were strong Godly laymen. They did not want the English to continue to rule over their new colonies. The founding fathers were in a total debate for several weeks drafting these two important documents. Their extended debate was regarding the content and wordage. They realized the importance of getting these right. These two documents became a permanent part of the founding father's instructions to all the people living in the new country called The United States of America. These written instruments have been a lasting standard by which we have operated since our Nation's inception. These have stood the test of time for over two hundred years. They remain the standard for most of the people who are tax paying citizens of our great country, although there are some people now questioning whether we still need to abide by these ordinances. A few believe there might be a better way. They want to pursue a different direction. They believe two hundred plus years is not enough proof that these still work. Some who want changes wish for even more government controls. Do these few individuals really know what they are asking for? Or, another good way to put it is, "Be careful what you ask for."

P. S. The U.S. Constitution and The Bill of Rights are still a sound standard for us today. "Yes, we need to be careful what we ask for, as well as, also, who we vote for."

PART 3: Two USA Documents

Some of the more famous members of the group who drafted those two important, historical documents, both the U.S. Constitution and The Bill of Rights, include Thomas Jefferson, John Hancock, Benjamin Franklin, James Madison, Patrick Henry, and Samuel Adams just to name six of the original fifty-six.

When the first pilgrims came over from the old country, history tells us, it was to get away from the government tyranny, just one of the many reasons was the government's mandate on how they were to practice their religion. These pilgrims wanted the freedom to worship their God in a way that they choose. They went at great risk to themselves and their families to secure passage and move to a place they had never seen, but had only heard of. The lessons we can learn from these people who first came over are the following. We should never take our freedoms for granted. We only have to look at other countries who do not allow the freedoms we still have available to us.

I believe we need to continue to educate our young to see the differences between what freedoms we have here and what others lack in other parts of the world. Are we being miss led to believe that the lack of freedom is a good thing, even when these changes take away what we had, and replace them with mandates dictated by those who govern over us?

One of the famous founding fathers, Thomas Jefferson, wrote the following sentence in one of his letters, "When the people fear the government there is tyranny, but when the government fears the people there is liberty."

I believe we are sitting too close to the dangerous edge of this subject. So many of our citizens now have a great fear of what our government will do next. These leaders were elected to do the People's Will, however, so many of these same leaders have been there so long that they appear to have forgotten the reason why they were elected. The original document starts off with these words, "We The People." Have we already gone too far away from what those fifty-six brave men drafted and signed? Can we go back to the way they wanted us to continue to run the country of and by the people? Can we still have a true return to those words, "Life, Liberty and the pursuit of Happiness? Please let me know what you think.

PART 4: Social Security

1. During his time in office, President Roosevelt put in place the Nation's Social Security system. It was started on August 14, 1935. It was structured so a small part of each worker's weekly income was withheld to provide for a retirement income for when these workers were in their senior years. It seemed like a good idea at the time. Up until that time, families and/or church families took care of aging family members. With this new plan, individuals could secure their own future for themselves by going with this new government retirement plan. It does work to a faction, however what they should have done when they started this program was to make it optional to individuals to go with the proposed government run plan, or allow a self-managed, individual, private plan. Both types would have to be overseen by the government, or reported to the government. However, the individual, private plans could be invested in any self-managed monetary fund that the individual might choose. Both the government plan and the private plan could be exempt from income tax on the earnings until the funds were drawn out upon retirement. The private plan would allow more flexibilities. It would be self-managed and all funding, also called contributions, would be the sole asset of the individual. This would mean the balance remaining in the retirement account at his or her death would become part of their estate and would be passed along to heirs of the estate. While with the government plan the family gets a total of $250.00 to help with burial expenses. There is no other money from the government retirement plan available to be passed along to the heirs of the estate.

2. Unlike the government social security investment fund, the individual's account could not be touched by the government. While the money in the government controlled Social Security Retirement Fund has been depleted for years, first during President Lyndon Johnson's time at the White House. The government borrowed from this government managed fund to help support the cost of the War in Vietnam. Later government thefts occurred again during President Reagan's time in office and lastly during President George W. Bush's time in office. The total amount taken during these three periods was 2.85 trillion dollars, leaving a balance in the fund of ZERO!! There are now three separate IOU from our Federal Government in place of the funds. The money is all gone, which means the withholding from present-day individual paychecks partially covers funds needed, while the remainder comes straight out of the Federal General Revenue collected monthly.

It should be noted that if any private company took funds out of their own employee's retirement fund, someone in senior management of that company would go to jail until restitution has been made.

3. Another interesting note, if we had any number of private retirement plans in place of the government managed plans, there would be huge dollars reinvested in stocks and bonds to grow companies, as well as, to invest in all sorts of profitable projects.

Further, the owners of these individual retirement account plans would have started contributing at the same time as if they started their original plan in a government run social security plan. Their contributions to their own personal retirement plan would have started from their very first paycheck, and in every pay day until their retirement. The total accumulated value in their plan will vary based upon the amount invested along with how long their designated retirement fund is in existence. With time and with compounding of interest and dividends, and with growth the total balance at retirement, it could be a much greater amount than what that same individual would have contributed to the government managed plan from his or her pay role withholdings.

Also a reminder, unlike the government plan, the individual, self-managed plan, any remaining balance at his or her death could have become part of their estate and left to their heirs.

4. These mandated, self-managed, retirement funds could have been invested in any number of plans, from bank deposits, to mutual funds, to treasury notes, precious metals, and beyond. Imagine if you and I each had somewhere above a quarter of a million dollars in our own self-managed retirement accounts accumulated over the years at your retirement. These could be enough to allow us to leave all of the unused retirement funds to our loved ones when we pass on. By comparison, only a small token in the government social security plan is left to our loved ones, which will pay only a very small part of our final burial expenses.

PART 5: Welfare System

We must address another socially designed program. This is our present welfare system. The first aid to the poor project started when none other than the same President Roosevelt backed it during the mid-1930s. It's not clear if these welfare changes prompted the change in income tax withholdings for the social security retirement plan, but they both came about at that same time period. The annual amount spent on welfare to the poor back then is not found, but we do have records for recent times. The total payment given out in welfare aid in 2016 was $729 billion, while 2017 totals were $732 billion. These welfare totals amount to about 20% of the total annual Federal expenditures for each of these two years. Which is close to one quarter of the total annual revenue our Nation takes in from the collection of our taxes. The above information was found on google. We make the assumption that these numbers are accurate.

> In this welfare program it seems we reward some for their mistakes, and for not being willing to go out and gain employment. We give support money to those who get themselves in a family way without the means to support themselves, and for couples who are not working, either because they haven't found employment, or are not inclined to go out and support themselves. We provide funding for rent, food, medical expenses, and all other needs through this program.

Prior to this new welfare program option in the 1930s the families took care of their own, or the people simply went out to find work to support themselves. In some cases the churches stepped in to provide some temporary help.

My first question, should it be the government's duty to take the place of family, or churches to support people in trouble in these cases? Shouldn't we find a way for the individuals to help themselves by finding them work, or for their families to come to their aid? Why are we rewarding them for their mistakes or for their lack of ability to support themselves?

Looking back at what the founding fathers drafted, we don't find anything to tell us yea or nay on this issue. I believe common sense should be used in these matters. Wouldn't it be more practical to help them find employment instead of just handing them our tax money month after month without any alternate plan? This welfare program might continue funding people month after month, and even year after year for generations for some as it is in some families.

Our system and our history in this long running welfare program is neither a good thing, nor is it helpful to any of the people involved, as well as, to us tax payers who pay the bills.

That old saying, "Give someone a fish every day, or teach them how to fish so they can help themselves." My question, are we taxpayers supposed to take care of every person who is not willing to take care of themselves? Looking at the numbers shown above, it's apparent this nanny state program is sucking up big chunks of our tax dollars. And, we see no one coming up with appropriate answers, except for some legislators calling for even more tax dollars to be spent in this program.

I read in the Bible, God's Holy Word, these words, "If a man is not willing to work, neither shall he eat." This sounds like a cold, inhumane statement, but it comes directly from God. Who am I to argue with the One who created all we see?

4. Should we go even further in our giveaway programs? Should we be offering these same welfare benefits to those who are here illegally? To those who are not citizens of our great Nation? There are different circumstances for these, some stole across our open borders in the dark of night, while others came with work or student visas, and then overstayed when their visas expired. Those who are without written authorization, do we send them all home? What is your answer to this question? We have many varying differing opinions on this one matter alone, not to mention all the other matters to be considered.

PART 6: Our Nation's Borders

In the last paragraph of part five, I briefly reference our Open Borders. The first question we must ask is how many other countries have these same immigrant conditions? And, are they having the same types of problems we here in the USA see happening today? The real answer is a profound "YES." We see the same or worse problems in other countries such as England, Germany and France, just to name three. Most of these countries allowed great numbers of refugees into their countries without much screening or vetting being done. But here in our own country some of our domestic problems continue because of our unprotected borders. We can't screen those who steal across our border undetected in the middle of the night. We have little idea how many of these who invade our territory are radicalized and come in with the intent to do harm, to steal, destroy or even to kill.

We have been fortunate that more chaos has not happened. Still, we have too many of our citizens who live in fear for what might happen, and too many others who have already been harmed or killed as a direct result. It could get much worse unless we can fully secure our sovereign borders, and then hopefully resolve the existing serious problems with all who are already here.

1. We need to develop a plan which will answer most of the problems we are experiencing as the result of our open borders. Some certain answers can come with some compromises by the leadership in our country working together. This author considers this our highest priority to secure the borders as quickly and effectively as possible. When that is completed, we must then come to some workable agreement of how to deal with all who remain here without proper documents. I don't advocate across the board amnesty as some might call for, however, it is going to take a lot of compromise by those who decide what can be done. I believe there are many still here after seven or more years who are gainfully employed, lawful, self-supporting individuals and families.

These should be able to stay, if they meet the following criteria. If they have not been a financial burden to us during the last seven years or more; if they fully pay the correct amount of taxes, and they have not been in trouble with the law for all the time that they have been here. These people are an asset to our Nation. I believe we can justify granting them citizenship because they do meet these conditions. Those here less than seven years, yet are fully employed, are not supplemented with our tax dollars, and have not been law breakers, or have not had problems with our laws should qualify for a temporary visa or green card dated from when they came across, and expiring a full seven years from that date. They can then be set up for a date to be granted citizenship, provided they are still employed, if they pay all taxes due, and have not been in trouble with the law.

1. However, those here illegally who remain a drain on our tax system, who may have had troubles with the law and/or who continue to lack financial support for their own households are a liability to us, and these must be returned back to their home country. Once we have secure borders, it will be very difficult for these to trespass back in under cover of darkness.

2. It is certain we do not have sufficient funding to continue to subsidize living costs for any non-citizens. Paying for food, housing, schooling, and medical services to those here illegally are not only foolish, but it is like dangling a carrot in front of the faces of all those from other lands who might want to steal across our open borders in hopes of being offered all these freebies. These funds can then be used for temporary help for our own citizens who fall on hard times, rather than helping all who are not supposed to be here to start with? If the undocumented are not paying their own way, then they are here at a great expense to all our tax paying citizens.

PART 7: Roe vs Wade

We now need to bring up another very controversial subject. And I'm puzzled as to why it is so much so. We all call ourselves civilized human beings. We feel we are mostly also considered very sympathetic, compassionate people. But, how can we as civilized and compassionate people justify the deliberate killing of another human being? How can we condone such an act, either personally, or even as a Nation. Why would we allow such a violent act upon another innocent, defenseless, tiny human being?

1. The U. S. Supreme Court came to a landmark ruling. In 1973 their ruling making it the law of the land. You're right, I'm speaking about the court's abortion ruling sent down on January 22nd, 1973 from our Nation's Highest Court. The Roe versus Wade ruling came to be on that date, and since that date more tiny American human beings have been intentionally killed than in all the wars since the United States signed our United States Declaration of Independence nearly two and one half centuries ago. Call it what you want to justify your belief, all those babies were alive, and were denied the opportunity to life when they were violently removed from their mother's womb. It was a life and was there. There was a heartbeat after only three or four weeks from conception. There was ten fingers and ten toes; two arms and two legs and every other characteristic of a human child in the first trimester. But

then, a decision was made for the unborn baby to be violently torn from the mother's womb.

Yet another shocking news report during the week of February 2nd, 2019 came out from the State of New York. Their change amended their abortion law to make it legal to terminate the unborn child (baby) right up until the moment of birth. What is even harder to believe, after that ruling was passed, some of their state leaders were celebrating this amendment in the Governor's office. The man who holds the highest office within the State of New York was there to celebrate, justifying the killing a fully developed child who is ready to come out and breathe the air we all get to breathe. Where are the compassions and civil human standards in that? It's truly hard to not judge others, when we hear of an educated, polished elected official who pledged to serve choosing to celebrate such an inhumane, violent action?

1. The next question, who is next on this list of the expendables? I'm seventy-seven years old. I'm semi-retired. Some would call me not gainfully employed. If I should live a few more years, will I and my peers be next on this termination list? I know there are some states who have already passed laws that allow the medical community to take the life of someone who makes the choice to die. They honor that person's request. But, is there a day coming when the state will make that decision for anyone

who is no longer a productive citizen? God forbid that this should happen. We appear to be one step away from that possibility today.

There is the reference in God's Holy word that a certain group of people actually sacrificed their young to the god of Moloch. They heated iron arms up and placed their live children on these arms as a means of worship or sacrifice to their god. I see no difference in what we are doing today, except we are doing it behind closed doors as a means to eliminate an unplanned inconvenience, and not as a means of worship. We deny the right to life for the most innocent, vulnerable, and the defenseless only because that child was there at a most inconvenient time. Some call it Pro-choice, or a Woman's Right to Choose, but what choice does the little innocent child still in the womb get in this matter?

Let's change and undue this ruling now state by state under the provisions given by the Tenth Amendment granted to each sovereign right. Let's make sure we don't lose someone who might one day find the real cure for some of the most dreaded, life-threatening diseases just because they were denied the right to be born. They were destroyed when they showed up at a most inconvenient time. The one who should have been there to nurture the innocent chose to end the life of their own child, often right up to the time the baby was to be delivered in birth.

PART 8: Leadership

1. The next subject also breaks my heart. It has gone on ever since God first allowed His people to have a king in place of His judges. This is still the case today, and it is sad to see the extent of corruption at almost every level of present-day government. It shows up when we hear leaders call good evil and evil good. When we see leaders giving precedent to some groups who represent less than five percent of our population, with disregard for the will of the majority on various issues. These may be done out of favoritism or because of the threats received from such minority groups. Or when one party holds a grudge match against the other party, or any single members of the other party, and even when the will of the people are adversely affected by these vendettas. Many of these same leaders fall in line with the socialistic ideas of free medical care for all. As well as open borders and opening our monetary treasures to all, including those who lack documents to prove citizenship, and then making our cities and states sanctuary safe havens for any undocumented alien in our midst.

2. Then, when our supposedly unbiased news people show favoritism to some people or issues, and then show and report only negative reports about others they disagree with. Note, not all of the news media companies do this, but enough do, which results in swaying the opinions of many people listening to and believing their biased reports. This condition has likely always been with us, however, it used to be all but undetectable years ago. But not so in today's reporting world. It is almost blatant. It is sad to see that many of the news stories are purposely designed to tell we the people what the reporting agency wants us to hear, versus what's true, and accurate, and then not revealing, or omitting all or some of the actual pertinent facts in each story reported.

May God help them to start doing what is right, and not what demonstrates partiality in all of each separate report.

3. Our people must demand the truth, the whole truth and nothing but the truth. It's my belief that biased, proven, false reporting should be considered a criminal act, subject to justice being done to any violators. I know the original documents also gave us freedom of the press. However, it appears that this is one right that the founders didn't take into consideration. They might never have considered things would ever get this seriously unbalanced. These, along with what is happening with some of the big tech, social media, and private companies are doing to censor our individual rights of freedom of speech through their public forms? This may not be illegal activity, but it also has proven to be totally without balance, because only one group of people are being censored. Even our last president was removed permanently from their services, even prior to him leaving the office of the presidency. I find this to be uncalled for, and inexcusable. It is enough so that those who intentionally block anyone's freedom of speech, protected in Amendment one of the U. S. constitution. It is without just cause and should be recognized by the appropriate authorities to be considered injustice and should be considered criminal acts, subject to persecution.

PART 9: Departure from Faith

1. The crumbling of our schools started in the sixties with the removal of prayers in schools. Then the next year they also removed teaching of the Holy Bible. In 1980 further removal of anything of God, was the removal of the Ten Commandments, or any reference to God at many of our institutions of learning. Then beyond that they began to push their ideas of "A separation of church and State." They took a letter Thomas Jefferson wrote about not wanting the State to interfere with the activities of the church and twisted it, spun it, to mean the church should not interfere with the State. This worked on behalf of their plan, to the unfortunate determinant of the Christian Church. The above mentioned changes also filtered down through every level of government, not just our schools. Their decision was based upon secular reasoning countering the reference in the First Amendment's protection of the rights of our people in the establishment of religious worship.

1. The eventual results of these changes have been tragic and disastrous. Respect and honor of our fellow human beings were lost when prayer ended in our places of education. Whether you are a Christian or not, you cannot argue with the value of prayer when it teaches us the importance of values, as well as, of what is right and wrong. The value of these two things cannot be overstated. We believe the event, the Columbine School killings, along with so many more similar tragedies that have happened, came about because we removed compassionate teaching in our public schools and in places of higher education. We then put in place some additional studies like sex ed, and in the later years instilling questions regarding what each individual student's gender is. Some people today are even trying to convince school administrations to establish unisex restrooms in our schools. This is still another step to crumble

our present-day school systems. These regressions have also crept into our society beyond the schools as well. We hear of moves to eliminate any references to gender on the floor of the U. S. congress. We see such a disregard in some areas for others in many communities.

When we take compassionate teaching away from the very young, it then stays with them when they are out there in the adult world. Not too many years ago we were taught to address those in authority with high regard. Maybe, if we didn't like how he or she administered their job, then it was done only because of the position he or she held. As an example, years ago we were taught to address our Nations President as "Mr. President," and our elected leaders by their titles followed by their last names. Today, that doesn't happen except in a few cases. Case in Point, President Obama was referred to by many as just, "Obama." Even our news media often refers to our current president by only his last name. This has certainly changed and has been carried forward to all the other areas of our lives.

3. To summarize: God speaks of His love for each of us. In the scripture, John 3:16 "God so loved the world that He gave His only Son that whosoever believes in Him will not perish but have eternal life."

For most of us our past records speak for themselves. We start off by doing well, but its how we finish that is really important. Today there are those people among us who find parts of the Bible and much of its content as hate speech. There are apparently many scriptures which they find offensive, even hateful. These have to do with fornication, adultery, idol worship and homosexuality. I reference only a couple of these here. You can decide if they are, in your own opinion, hate speech. The first, Ephesians 5:5 "For this you know, that no fornicator, unclean person, nor covetous man, who is an idolater, has any inheritance in the kingdom of Christ and God." And the next one, "1 Corinthians 6:9-10 "Do you not know that the unrighteous will not inherit the kingdom of God? Do not be deceived, neither adulterers, nor homosexuals, nor sodomites, nor thieves, nor covetous, nor drunkards, nor revilers, nor extortioners will inherit the kingdom of God."

These are clear words that tell us not to live in such a way. But, the truth is, if you have any one of the above conditions in your life you have only to turn away from them with a repentant heart, and then ask God to forgive you. And, the good news is He will gladly do that. The Bible calls it being cleansed from all unrighteousness.

PART 10: Fairer Taxation

This part is about various current federal and state income tax methods. The Lord told us in the Holy Scriptures in Mark 12:17 "Render unto Caesar the things that are Caesar's and to God the things that are God's." He also instructed us to pray for those in authority over us. This gives us some good direction on how we are supposed to conduct our lives. We see much that we would like to change in our country. One of these is the current income tax code. We are not advocating avoiding paying the taxes due to our state and federal governments, however, we do see much that could be changed and corrected in the method to make a tax system more fair to all citizens. For years we have had some imbalances. First we label, the marriage penalty tax, for lack of a better title. It makes a married couple filing jointly pay more in tax than two non-married people living together, if they file separately when all other conditions and incomes are similar.

The next thing is the huge document called the tax code. It's 70,000 plus pages of rules and regulations covering every aspect of how we are to make up our tax returns. I mean, come on! Who can understand and live with such a monster? It makes it almost impossible to follow all the in's and out's to interpret every point that is in the existing tax code. I know that those who have businesses have their sections and file under that status. But, come on! I'm going to be brief, just one or two pages at the most should be sufficient to tell what we need to follow in instruction to file each year. I believe we can improve what is there now. I've read about the various options for ideas on how

we can truly simplify the tax code. I've also considered each from not

just the taxpayer point of view, but also from the government's position.

I find only one new system that makes sense from all POV. (Points

of view) That method is the Fair Tax Plan. It's simple, economically

sound, and it saves everyone money. It will also make heroes out of

all elected leaders who push to pass this plan. The following are the

advantages: It eliminates the need for all individual filings; it brings back

huge investment dollars now being invested overseas; it cuts the cost

of our government payroll; it levels the field for all taxpayers; it makes

our local goods and services more competitive in both the domestic and

world market place; all, but the very poor, are equal in carrying the tax

load; it collects taxes due at the point of sale for all, including tourists

visiting our country; it reduces the possibility of tax fraud; it lowers the

cost of living for all when it eliminates the embedded tax in all new

products sold; it saves time and cost of record keeping for all; it saves

trees; it saves all of us from the worry about some part of the current tax

code we might have missed when we file the current required tax returns

each year; and it makes April 15th just another wonderful spring day to

enjoy and to go about our daily lives.

I would like to see each State and Federal Congressperson and Senator look long and hard, with an open mind, at all the benefits shown above, and then I encourage you all to get together with your peers and put forth a plan to change both the State and Federal tax code to this Fair Tax Plan. Or, at least give us some just reason why you will not consider this plan for the people you have pledged to represent and serve. <u>You will be our heroes</u> if you and your fellow leaders will work together to get this accomplished.

PART 11: Love for our Neighbors

This part is about race. The first big question is, "Why can't we all decide to just get along?" Then the second, isn't there enough division here within our country now that we go out of our way to deal poorly with any of our neighbors?

God's word is clear. Jesus shared this with His disciples about the two greatest commandments found in the Holy Bible in the book of Matthew 22:37-40 ""You shall love the Lord your God with all your heart, with all your soul, and with all your mind. This is the first and greatest commandment. And second is like it: You shall love your neighbor as yourself. On these two commandments hang all the Law and the Prophets."

Not too many years ago someone came up with the saying, "Black lives matter." My answer is, "OF COURSE BLACK LIVES MATTER! But, so do all other lives matter." Some of the nicest people I've met are of a different color than me, but did the color of their skin make a difference for me. No! The heart of the matter is what is in their heart. How they treat others. How they have compassion for anyone, yes anyone who has a need. We are instructed to have compassion for others when we see they are hungry, thirsty or in need of any other reasonable necessity, and we have the ability to help them. This was more the way people were a half-century ago.

I remember years ago when one of our neighbor farmers ended up in the hospital during the grain harvest time. Many of our neighbors got together to save this man's crops by pulling their machines in and harvesting the crops for him and his family. They had a need and many came together to help out. It didn't matter what his politics was, or the color of his skin. It was that he had a need and many came to his rescue. Why can't we, you and I, follow this same example for those who live in our own neighborhoods, no matter the color of their skin, or their politics? Can we justify the simple rule, "Love your neighbor no matter what?"

Final Conclusion of this Writer:

Our country, The United States of America, has been known around the world as a beacon of freedom and liberty for our citizens for more than two and one third centuries. We have certainly maintained that status going forward for most of that time, after we sent the British packing for home after we defeated them, gaining our total independence back in the late 1700s.

Following that time in history, we have certainly made some occasional wrong turns here and there which slowed us up, but until recently, we have been able to correct our course to avoid complete failure. We have tried to be the world police force, as well as, its peacemaker. Both world wars are two prime examples of our attempts to use peaceful diplomacy first, before involving the strength of our might to bring an end to the tyranny of a mad man who was bent on taking over the whole world. He came too close to doing just that after taking over most of Eastern Europe, and making too much progress in Western Europe as well. Their goal was also to try to wipe out a certain group of people.

This man's whole military plan had some startling successes until we became actively involved at the war front. The only way we found to stop him was through our great strength, and the combined collation with many of our European allies. Even then, Hitler's forces and military might were difficult to put down.

It was during our efforts in the western European front that Japan decided to invade our Pacific assets. They felt we were an easy target with much of our strength involved overseas in Europe. We then were in two different war fronts, both in Europe and the Pacific. History shows we were successful, however, it was at great cost in precious lives, as well as, huge monetary costs. War has proven to be a terrible way to prove one's strength.

Several years later we were in a cold war status with the USSR, a big part of it is now known as Russia. I remember a recorded conversation between our then President Ronald Reagan and the USSR leader Mr. Gorbachev. Part of their talk involved the possibility of either one of the two Nations ever using atomic weapons against one another. Mr. Gorbachev indicated that they have no need to do this as we, in our country, will eventually implode from within.

Both Mr. Reagan and Mr. Gorbachev are no longer still alive. But one has to wonder if what Mr. Gorbachev had said to President Reagan back then is now quickly happening right in front of our eyes.

So far, our present day conflicts are for the most part of a different nature. They are mostly internal domestic words of war regarding differences between those of us who love this Nation and have an appreciation for all those who first founded our Republic, with those who are determined to radically change how we have lived for these many years. There are those who want to take away our precious freedoms of speech, right to carry guns, freedom of life, liberty and the pursuit of happiness. They are fewer in numbers, but are ruthless in their efforts.

We give honor to all of those who have spent their all to defend all these precious freedoms and liberties we enjoy. We can't allow these to be taken away without standing up for our rights given us by the famous documents our Founding Fore Father's drafted on our behalf all those years ago, and by those who fought to protect our freedoms and liberties.

So far, our present internal domestic conflicts have mostly been only a war of words about differing agendas or ideals. But, these are no easier to fight for because it involves persuading others to change their minds through common bonds and through common sense for what is best for all of our people's future. For the most part no guns or Braun have been needed in this war of words, except for some frequent riotous activities in parts of some of our larger cities who have been under siege, and subject to destruction, burning and looting during the past several months by many anti-American groups.

Webster defines the word "Republic" as, 1. "A political order in which the power is held by elected representatives of its citizens." 2. "A Nation with such a political order."

Today there are some who want our government to have more power, or even have total control over our lives. They are pushing for a socialistic society where the government provides for our all, and where we will have no say in how we are governed. In more than one of the parts above, I explained that every experiment with total government control over its people has proven to be a complete failure. It leads to a collapse of the social structure of the country. Many examples are available. The Soviet Union was one. Also, even more recent is all what Venezuela is currently going through to recover. Cuba and North Korea are two that have lasted the longest, but if you look at the people, the masses in these two countries are not doing very well with one man, or a small group controlling all the wealth and even the substance in their countries.

I get angry when I see what a small number of people here who are trying to force feed their radical, leftist views upon us. Even some of the private, and public news sources are promoting their same language. The numbers who want these radical changes are small in comparison to the headcount of our countries whole population. But, with the help of some of our news agencies, they are pushing a takeover of the whole Nation with their leftist agenda. And they have gain a big part of the news platform spreading a false narrative around the country helping them. These leftist groups are hell-bent on moving our Nation into a country controlled by a very small number of leaders. It feels like they are attempting to destroy our Nation from within. Their agenda is not with arms and force like the mad man who tried to take over all of Europe and beyond. But their methods, with their ideas and policies of persuasion that control and deceive the minds of our future leaders are to transform our Nation into something other than what the rest of us are trying to preserve today. Their plan, their agenda, started with all those government giveaway programs, making us more and more dependent on Uncle Sam to take care of us. Then further conditioning our citizens to become more and more dependent on the government to provide for whatever they may want or need. Later we find that it converts us into a society that expects the government to take care of us from birth until death. We simply cannot let them succeed. Yet a small number have convinced some of our twenty-something age groups through academic means that these socialistic ideas are credible. Some of these most radical ideas, which, if we allow them to be successful in bringing into place, will destroy our country as we know it today, and they might do it without ever firing a shot. We need to quickly remind all others of the history of other countries where a dictatorship was brought to play, and then show our fellow citizens how many of those countries have failed, or are on the verge of failure. When their government falls into chaos they leave their people in a terrible condition from which many do not survive because of lack of employment and looting and riotous activities. We need to avoid moving our own country towards a government with total control. And we need to do that now, and at all cost.

Beyond that we need to apologize to our children and grandchildren for allowing our elected leaders to create the huge debt our States and Federal Governments have run up. Debts created to fund their foolish spending programs, many that should have never been done by our government. Many of these we have had in place for a long time. Most of these which should have been the responsibility of individual family members, or maybe even temporary help from our houses of worship.

Our present and past leaders have found, and continue to find so many ways to spend our tax dollars on new untested programs. Many of these will be, or are currently funded with borrowed moneys creating further indebtedness. They are spending our children and grandchildren's future paychecks as they borrow more and more money to keep them running.

When our Federal government tapped into the Social Security Retirement funds the very first time back in the Lyndon Johnson Administration during the 1960s, we should have called them on that practice. Their theft of moneys from our social security trust funds back then established a precedent which was later acted upon twice more leaving our Nation's Social Security retirement fund for all senior retirees empty. Today these benefits for retirees come in part from withholdings of people who are currently in the workforce, and the rest from our Nation's general fund which is our tax dollars which was originally pledged and designed for the operation of the rest of our government. How much longer will the government be able to borrow more money? Is there an end game in sight to pay these funds back without loading the payback upon our own children and grandchildren? What can you and I do as private citizens to persuade our leaders to change course before we implode financially from within?

I offer some doable solutions:

The federal tax system originated during the early 1900s as a temporary tax to fund the cost of the First World War. But the federal tax requirement never went away.

We now seriously need to make some changes to that plan to help both our tax payers, as well as, our government. I've recommended we move to the Fair Tax Plan, also called a consumption tax plan, replacing the current state and federal income tax systems that were put in place, and then added to over the many years. This new Fair Tax Plan would be based upon a percentage of the amount of new purchases, or consumption versus the current percentage of individuals and businesses annual income. When passed it will bring back huge investment dollars now being kept overseas because of our high capital gains tax on income. It will give 'We the People' power to decide how much tax we each pay based upon our own spending instead of on our income. And it will not be subject to some percentage of our income as our governments determine. This alternative plan is called Fair Tax for a good reason. It allows all of us to help support the operation of our governments, leveling the playing field for all. It will all but eliminate tax fraud, which is, for the most part, people who fail to report some or all of their taxable annual income. It will make April 15th just another beautiful April day

to enjoy. And, it will save all those trees that now go to provide all the

paper we use to file our tax each quarter, and at the end of each tax

year. Other benefits are it lowers the cost of our purchases because it

removes all embedded tax from each purchase of new products, and it

will eliminate withholding from each paycheck, both of which will make

the amount on our paychecks go up. Still another benefit, it will make

our countries products and services more competitive in the world trade

market place.

> Next, we need to reopen up oil and natural gas exploration
> on all the undeveloped federally own lands, excluding any
> improved federal properties such as parks and recreational
> areas. This reopening will make the USA continue to be the
> world's biggest supplier of oil and natural gas, which is the
> primary commodity used around the world for energy
> sources. Then we should use the larger portion of the money
> collected from sales of oil and gas from public lands to pay
> towards our Nation's huge indebtedness.

> Next we need to fully secure our borders. Stop, or at least slow
> down, the movement of illegals from coming in under dark
> of night, or from over staying their student or work visas. It
> will also make it much more difficult to smuggle illegal drugs,
> as well as, the human trafficking activities coming here for
> whatever harms and burdens they cause.

Further, we should register all who come in both under work and student visas so that we can track them when their visa expires, making enforcement actions easier and finding them when it does become necessary.

Also, we must stop subsidizing non-citizens, giving support money, housing, schooling, and medical benefits to any undocumented, non-citizens. This also will include revising all of our current welfare programs to set up programs to train potential future workers from any of these groups. Our goal should be to require them to gain full employment to support themselves and their families.

Then we need to further revise the federal and state annual budgets to reduce each department's spending by 1% each year until they no longer spend more tax money than they take in. Further we should evaluate and revise all other spending programs in our effort to improve budgeting of how our tax dollars are spent. The rule of thumb should always be to spend only to qualified places where it will make both the recipient and the government the better for spending these funds. Roads and infrastructure, along with police, our border protection, and our fine military who protect us from enemy evasions are some prime examples of good and necessary government spending. Even these might be modified to save funds by letting supply and demand dictate labor and material costs. No more using extraordinarily high hourly prevailing wage dollars, and no more $200.00 hammers. If you know what I mean.

With the above changes we can work towards the needed improvements in how we operate within our financial budgets. We have many highly intelligent money experts already on payroll at each level of our governments. Why not use these experts to budget, and to gain control of every aspect of our government's operations including our spending.

May I give you an example of foolish spending? Where I was the recipient, beneficiary, in this one case. This happened many years ago. I was a window covering contractor for almost twenty years. I received a contract to furnish and install draperies and track in 72 rooms in each of the three new non-officer barracks buildings on the Travis Air Force base, Fairfield, California. I was told to order the materials, which were draperies and curtain track hardware, for these, which I did. I arranged to ship them to the project location. Shortly before I was about to start installation I received a change order that changed the product to mini blinds in place of the draperies and track for all three buildings. I submitted my quote for the change order, and it was quickly approved. So, I ordered the mini blinds and installed them as soon as the project was ready for them.

I later asked the contractor what was to be done with the original drapery and track materials. He informed me that they were to be held in storage on the base. I was paid for both the original materials, and for the mini blinds, along with the installation of them. It appeared to me that our tax money spent on the original materials may have been wasted. I hope that they found a place to use these, and that they are not still being stored there all these years later. It leaves a person to wonder how many similar cases have been done that we may never know about.

Yet another story is as follows. I remember seeing a TV special broadcast, about three or four years ago. This report showed of dozens of vacant, empty federally owned buildings in various parts of our country. Several of these buildings had been empty for years. The cost to acquire, and then to maintain these unused buildings could be in the untold millions, or maybe even billions of dollars. If this news report was accurate, couldn't these buildings be sold off to recover some of our tax dollars? It leads one to wonder is there anyone watching the store? Who is guarding the till and safeguarding our investments? Is the government we have way more than we need?

I prayerfully leave you to dwell on all of these questions. I also encourage you to write to your elected leaders often when you see any abuse of the authority that we give them. If we don't act upon what we know is done in error, then they will take the liberty to do even more things that are detrimental to our Nation's wellbeing. It's up to each of us to hold these leaders accountable, that is, if they want to continue to receive our votes come reelection time.

My promised final summary:

We should give our current leaders one hundred days into their new elected position to right some of the wrongs that cause the overspending that's threatening our country's economic survival. We need to get them to understand the dire urgency for making these corrections. Should they continue on without showing some sign of change/correction, and then follow up with vast improvements, then we must control the purse strings, control how much of our money is sent to the U. S. Treasury. We do have some controls by first finding willing candidates who actively work towards a balanced budget, then wait until the next election to replace the other candidates who are not willing to work on budget restraints. If waiting for the next election is not quick enough for the many of us, then we can quietly go as employees to our employers to increase our total exemptions to ten for a period of six to nine months, then save back that money so we can pay the tax due come April next year. Self-employed people can just reduce their estimated tax payment down to 10%. This change would have to be coordinated. If enough tax payers did this all at the same time for six to nine months our elected leaders will quickly get the message when the money going into the treasury slows down to a trickle. They will then see that they really don't have all the controls.

The next idea is to find a way to compete with all of our big tech companies. One possible way to let our numbers and our dollars speak for us. It will take some big money to start our own ride, namely a new internet service. If we, some one hundred million people who are unhappy with the censoring, are willing to donate a onetime donation of $10.00 to this cause, then see if we can convince our former President, or someone like him, to oversee the set-up of our new system. We could have another option in warp speed, much like he did with getting our vaccination process for Covid-19. Plus, considering what the old network did to censor him, it might be something he would be willing to put together. If we can get one hundred million contributions times $10.00 each. It might be enough to accomplish this project. Think of it, no more censoring of our speech, no more limiting our way to communicate with our Friends. Limitations in our freedom of speech approved by the First Amendment would be canceled.

God has blessed our great Nation. He has been long suffering with us in all the things we are doing that go against his will and His way.

Also we have been a good friend and an ally to the state of Israel for many years. However, if we chose to withdraw from them, and then continue to go against God's instruction for us, how much longer will He allow us to be a leader in good standing around the world?

We are to continue to have compassion for the poor, but not to continue to give when they show no sign of ever helping themselves. We should help and show love to our neighbors with the same mentality as to the poor. We should protect the very innocent with our all; giving honor to God, to our flag, and to our country. God told us to pray for all those who are in authority over us, and forgive others for their errors, so we can receive our own forgiveness.

My prayer, with God's guidance, that we can go back to the way that our brilliant Founding Fathers drew up the documents we have use to guide our country up until now. My hope is that others will come alongside of us and pray for our Nation and our leaders. God told us in His Word to pray without ceasing; to pray persistently for His will to be done, and to keep Him as our final authority over us.

Amen and amen.

Also by J. Gordon Monson (aka) Jim Monson

Did you love *Why? Are we Crumbling From Within?*? Then
you should read *The Bridge so Long*[1] by J. Gordon Monson!

tps://books2read.com/u/mYojpd

1. https://books2read.com/u/mYojpd

2

This book, The Bridge so Long, is a story about Spenser Madison, a
twenty something man with a very routine life, maybe even a very dull
life, until that one particular day when he was to take Mr. Able, his boss,
to catch a plane going to a conference. The short trip and the events
that took place before he could pick up his boss changed his whole life
from that moment on. He to quickly found out what ja difference just
one moment in time can make. He also found out that he needed help
from strangers to get out of the difficulties that came looking for him.
Many of these strangers eventually became good friends to Spencer. One
in particular, Emily, became much more than just a friend. How they met

and what she did to help him in his time of need is revealed in their story. I let Spenser tell this in his own words.

About the Author

Jim has been writing for many years going back to his early twenties. It is a passion of his, and because he was blessed with a vivid imagination, he enjoys producing fiction, both in first person and third person.

He also has a passion for what is going on within our country right now, and he feels we in our country need God's guidance to move forward from here.

---

[1] .https://en.wikipedia.org/wiki/Truism

[2] .https://en.wikipedia.org/wiki/United_States_v._Sprague

[3] .https://en.wikipedia.org/wiki/Supreme_Court_of_the_United_States

Did you love *Why? Are we Crumbling From Within?*? Then you should read *The Bridge so Long*[1] by J. Gordon Monson!

[2]

This book, The Bridge so Long, is a story about Spenser Madison, a twenty something man with a very routine life, maybe even a very dull life, until that one particular day when he was to take Mr. Able, his boss, to catch a plane going to a conference. The short trip and the events that took place before he could pick up his boss changed his whole life from that moment on. He to quickly found out what ja difference just one moment in time can make. He also found out that he needed help from strangers to get out of the difficulties that came looking for him. Many of these strangers eventually became good friends to Spencer. One in particular, Emily, became much more than just a friend. How they met

1. https://books2read.com/u/mYojpd

2. https://books2read.com/u/mYojpd

and what she did to help him in his time of need is revealed in the story. I let Spenser tell you his story in his own words.

About the Author

Jim has been writing for many years going back to his early twenties. It is a passion of his, and because he was blessed with a vivid imagination, he enjoys producing fiction, both in first person and third person.